"You Can't Fix What You Don't Know"

Learning Series

Fix Your Finances

Your Quick Tips Guide to Credit, Budgets, and Starting a Financial Plan

Jessica L ONeal

Copyright © 2018 – Jessica Oneal – All rights reserved.

No part of this book may be reproduced, distributed, or by any means, including photocopying, recording, or other electronic or mechanical methods without written permission of the publisher.

ISBN – 13: 978-1717001016

Internal Image Credits:
Money Bag –
https://pixabay.com/en/money-dollars-weights-ticket-2831248/
Credit card –
https://pixabay.com/en/bank-buy-card-credit-credit-card-1300155/
Paid –
https://pixabay.com/en/payment-black-white-921087/
Money in the air–
https://pixabay.com/en/money-dollars-raining-falling-down-2831324/
Balance –
https://pixabay.com/en/money-the-grace-of-the-weight-of-the-2033591/
Checklist –
https://pixabay.com/en/todo-list-terminal-board-check-off-2103511/

Dedication

To my children Martha, Omari, and Adrien... every day, I am more inspired by how amazing you are. I love you with all my heart.

Disclaimers and Terms of Use

This book is for informational purposes only. Everyone's financial situation and circumstances are unique. Your local municipality may also involve specific tax and credit rules, laws. or guidelines that could affect your financial matters. All readers accept and release the author and any affiliates from any liability or responsibility for any outcomes as a result of actions influenced by the contents of this book. All readers must accept full responsibility for any and all outcomes as a result of ideas implemented from this book or actions influenced by this book and agree to seek appropriate financial guidance from licensed, certified, or registered advisors before implementing any ideas or suggestions featured in this book. Readers should consult advisors including bankers, financial advisors, accountants, lawyers, insurance agents, or other professionals as required by your circumstances.

Any references to Trademarked names and entities is for editorial, reference, and/or informational purposes only. No recommendations or endorsements should be assumed. Likewise, no reference is intended to feature any entities in a derogatory way.

Table of Contents

How to Fix Your Finances	7
Chapter 1 – Improving Your Credit	9
Chapter 2 – Reducing Your Debt	15
Chapter 3 – Boosting Your Income	21
Chapter 4 – Balancing Your Budget	27
Chapter 5 – Making Your Financial Plan	33

How to Fix Your Finances

If the thought of credit, budgets, and financial plans makes you feel overwhelmed and stressed, you're not alone. Most people, even those that are very wealthy, experience anxiety when it comes to money issues. And financial matters are among the biggest reasons that couples disagree, argue, and breakup.

The good news is that this "quick-tips guide" was written to help you reduce your anxiety about credit, debt, budgeting, and financial planning, so you can finally fix your finances. We've cut out all of the confusing financial mumbo jumbo and complicated strategies to give you practical and painless ways to make the most out of your money.

Each section will focus on the best ways to fix your finances when it comes to improving your credit, reducing your debt, balancing a budget, boosting your income, and creating a financial plan. You may not be ready or able to follow all of the suggestions in this book. The key is to work on each section a little at a time and to keep working on making improvements to fix your financial stability. It all starts with taking that first step and making smart decisions about what is best for you and your family.

So, let's fix your finances!

Chapter 1
Improving Your Credit

Having credit is a benefit that allows you to secure some of life's most important necessities. Credit is necessary for the big things like buying a car or buying a home. It may be necessary if you apply for insurance, utility services, or a cell phone. It can also be a factor in whether or not you are hired for a job you want.

However, credit can also be the cause of financial ruin. Too much credit debt or credit mismanagement (such as late payments) can all have a negative impact on your finances. Overuse and misuse of your credit can quickly lead to financially damaging consequences.

The challenge is to build your credit, protect your credit reputation, and to use your credit wisely. Often, the biggest challenge to fixing one's finances involves fixing one's credit record. So, let's start with the basics and then look at the best ways to improve your credit.

What Is Credit?
Credit is simply the ability to make a purchase without paying for the item at the time of purchase. Either the party who is selling the item or a third-party lender is trusting you to make the payment as promised, in the future. The cost of having this credit is a percentage of the amount that is being loaned to you so that you can obtain something that you may not currently have the funds to purchase.

In most cases, it may be financial appropriate to use credit to buy a car or to buy a house. However, the trouble arises when we start to use credit for your day-to-day expenses. When we start to buy things on credit that we don't have the money to pay for, we very likely buy things that we really don't need or that we wouldn't buy if we had to pay cash for it. So, using credit for "the small things" usually results in more unnecessary spending. This creates more and more debt that would otherwise have been avoided. Having available credit often leads to unwise impulse purchases.

Your Credit Record
When a company such as a store or a bank issues you credit, they will report your payment record and balance history to credit reporting agencies. This is how companies that you ask to give you credit in the future, can determine if they should trust you with more credit.

If you do not have a credit history yet and need to build your credit record the best ways to do that include:

- You can become an authorized user on someone else's credit account. For example: if you have a family member who has good credit, they can add you as an authorized user to their credit account. Even if you do not use the account, the details about the management of the account will be reported to your credit record as well as the owner of the account. Keep in mind that if the account owner starts to mismanage their credit account, that negative information will also be added to your record. Likewise, if you do something to negatively impact that account, the account owner's record will also be tarnished.

- You can apply for a Credit-Builder Loan. Some banks and credit unions offer credit-builder loans. These are secured loan situations used to show a pattern of responsible repayment to build your credit history. The way it works is – you borrow a certain amount. The money is not disbursed to you. Instead it is held in a savings type of account to secure the loan. You then start to make payments to pay back the loan account. In essence it is like you are adding deposits to a saving account. However, the lender will report your payments as if you took possession of the loan value and are responsibly repaying. Once the full amount of the loan has been paid by you, you then receive your "payments" or saved funds. So, technically you made regular deposits into a "savings" account in a way that is reported as a "repayment" on a loan.

- You can apply for a secure credit card. Essentially what you do is deposit an amount with the credit card company that is equal to the amount of your credit. Your secure deposit serves as collateral to protect the lender in case of default. You then have an opportunity to build a credit history showing responsible use of your credit account and on-time payment habits.

Monitoring Your Credit
In order to protect your credit and monitor your financial reputation you should regularly check your credit record. There are 3 major credit bureaus that creditors use to report their customers' credit behavior and to check the credit of new customers who they are considering for credit accounts. Most of your credit information will be the same with all 3 bureaus.

It is possible that there could be differences and discrepancies. Not every credit card company or lender reports to all agencies. So, it is your responsibility to make sure that your credit record is correct with all 3 bureaus. You should also check regularly to protect yourself from identity theft. If someone is illegally using your credit and identity, it may be reflected on your credit report. If you see any accounts on your reports that you did not open, you should report it to the all 3 credit bureaus, to the Federal Trade Commission (877-382-4357), and then file a local police report.

The 3 credit bureaus may charge you for access to your credit report. However, you can get a free copy of your credit report once per year through: **http://AnnualCreditReport.com**.

Here is the contact information for the 3 main credit bureaus:

Equifax
https://www.equifax.com/personal/
1-800-525-6285

Experian
https://www.experian.com/
1-888-397-3742

TransUnion
https://www.transunion.com
1-800-680-7289
TransUnion also offers a free credit monitoring service, True Identity, to help you keep tabs on changes to your credit report. You can sign up at **https://www.trueidentity.com/**.

Your Credit Score
In addition to your credit report that shows your credit experience and behavior, lenders will also want to know your credit score before they decide to lend money to you or give you credit. The main source for credit scores is FICO. About 90% of the top lenders in the U.S. use FICO credit scores to determine if they should risk lending to you. The FICO score attempts to predict how likely you are to pay your bills on time and whether or not you are likely to repay the debt.

Your FICO score is determined by information gathered from your credit report. It evaluates your payment history, the type of credit you have, how long you have had various credit accounts, if you have recent or new credit obligations, and if you are at your limits or maxed-out on all of your credit accounts.

Improving Your Credit Report and Your Credit Score
The things that are most likely to help you improve your credit record and reputation include:

- Paying your bills on time

- Staying under 30% usage of your available credit. In other words, if you have a credit line of $100 do your best to not have an unpaid balance on the account that exceeds $30. Do your best to pay your balance in full every month. This is easiest if you only buy things that you have the cash on hand to pay for and immediately use those funds to pay the balance.

- The older your credit accounts the more they help your credit score. Newer debts are riskier for lenders. So, if you have an older account with a good payment record, keep it and keep paying on time. Your payment history and the age of your accounts is important.

- Keeping your credit accounts to a minimum. The more credit accounts you have and the more you owe, the lower your FICO score.

- Monitoring your credit reports for errors and accuracy. This will help to assure that your score is accurate and protect you from potential identity theft.

FICO scores range from 300 to 850. The higher your score the better your credit reputation. The lower your score, the lower the chances that you will be approved for additional credit. Your cost of credit, if approved, may also be higher if your score is low. To find out more about FICO scores and ways to improve them, go to **https://www.myfico.com**.

So, the best way to have good credit for the important things in life is to carefully build and protect your credit reputation with the small things. If you use your credit wisely, you are more likely to have the credit access you need, when you need it most.

Chapter 2
Reducing Your Debt

In the last chapter we talked about ways to improve your credit record which improves your chances of getting credit. But getting credit might not be your concern. Perhaps you have been so good at getting credit that you now want to reduce all of your debt.

There are a few things that you can do to reduce your debt faster, so less of your income goes straight to your creditors. Here are some of the best ways to get that debt balance down and your savings back up.

- Reduce your unnecessary expenses. Start to keep a journal of every dollar you spend and what you are spending it on. Keep your receipts and record each expense. This will help you to realize all of the money you spend that is a waste or really unnecessary. This will help you identify money that you could be saving and applying toward your bills to pay them off sooner.

- Create a budget. Many people think that creating a budget is a lot of work and resist the idea to pre-plan what their expenses and limits will be for a specific period of time – such as a month. However, creating a budget and sticking to it is easier than you realize and the benefits to your financial health are enormous. In Chapter 4, you'll learn some easy ways to create a budget. Give it a try to help you monitor your expenses and to make sure that your money is used on only important things. This will help you to save even more and reduce more of your debt. Spend less, save more, and use your savings to reduce your debt.

- Keep good records of your bills and due dates. Sometimes, sloppy recordkeeping causes people to forget to make payments which hurts your credit record and costs you more in late fees. Late fees add to your debt balances. So, stay organized and make your payments on time.

- Make a list of all of your bills from the ones with the largest balances to the lowest balances. Do your best to pay off the smallest one as soon as possible, paying your minimum required amount on all of the others. Once the smallest one is paid, you have one less monthly payment. Then use the extra money that you needed monthly to pay that smallest bill and apply it to the next smallest balance to pay that one off as soon as possible too.

This process of knocking off each of your smallest bills, one by one, can be very effective in reducing your overall debt accounts. Keep in mind that once you pay an account in full, you may benefit from keeping the account open with a zero balance, since the age of your credit accounts will influence your credit record and credit score.

- Ask for a lower rate. This doesn't always work but it is worth a try. You can ask your lenders, especially for collateralized debt such as a home loan, if they would modify your terms. They might consider this to ease your credit pressure and reduce the possibility that you might default on the debt altogether. Sometimes this effort could reduce your payments and/or reduce your interest rate. If you do receive modified terms, then use the savings to pay down other more-costly debt.

Fix Your Finances

- If you can pay more than the minimums, you should. By paying only the minimums, you drag your debt out for an excessive amount of time. This can be very costly, especially with high interest revolving credit accounts. The only time that paying, just the minimums, makes sense is when you are trying to payoff the smallest accounts one by one as mentioned earlier.

- Do an inventory of all of the stuff you just "had to have" so you used your credit to get it. Impulse buys can very quickly use up all of the available credit balance. It is hard to say "no" to the things we want when we have the ability to buy them – even if we are adding to our debt load. Sometimes impulse buying is fueled by the urge to take advantage of an awesome sale. The problem is that by the time you pay back the credit debt for that awesome sale item, you might discover that you paid 4 times as much in interest fees. That's not really a bargain, is it?

So, review all of those "must have" bargains. Do you now realize that you no longer play that video game, or use that fancy coffee pot that requires expensive coffee pods? Do you still wear those orange leggings? Can you sell any of that stuff on ebay, through a consignment shop, or Facebook Marketplace? A garage sale might also work. If you are able to raise some funds by selling the stuff you no longer want, then use the extra money, you get from selling, to reduce your debt.

- Don't tempt yourself. If you know that there's no way you can go to the mall without getting at least 1 thing, then don't go to the mall. All of those "1 things" add up to a lot of things that you didn't really need and wasted money on. You will quickly use up your available credit and add to your debt. It really helps when you are honest with yourself.

Even if you say you are only going to "window shop" you know that if you find a "must have" or a "super bargain" you won't be able to resist. The credit card will be out, and you'll be the proud owner of another thing you didn't really need that will eventually cost you 4 times as much by the time you really pay for it. If you do decide to go to places that you know will be tempting, take cash and leave the credit card at home. This way you will realize the exact amount that you are parting with when you make the purchase. You'll be less likely to spend "real money" in a wasteful way.

- Increase your income. Use your time and talent to make some extra money. One of the best ways to reduce your debt is to produce more income to pay off your balances. You may not have realized that this is even an option. In Chapter 3, you'll discover some interesting and creative ways to earn some more income to help you to fix your finances.

The important thing to remember when trying to reduce your debt, is that staying organized and focused on what you really need versus what you really want, will help you to minimize your wasted money that could be used to reduce your debt. And to really make a dent in your debt load, find your "side hustle" to raise some extra revenue that can be used to pay off your debts. More on that in the next section.

Chapter 3
Boosting Your Income

Sometimes your budget is so tight that there are very few ways, if any, to reduce more of your expenses. This means that the only way to improve your financial situation is if you are able to get more income. You may not realize all of the ways you can boost your income to improve your financial situation.

Change Jobs
The first place to start, is with your current job. This isn't always an option and there may be few opportunities for you to just change jobs for a higher salary. But do take the time to explore your options, prepare a resume, and keep a look out for opportunities that could improve your main source of income. Set up job notice alerts on websites such as Monster.com, CareerBuilder.com, LinkedIN.com, Indeed.com and SimplyHired.com. You may even discover that your current employer is advertising open positions that you didn't know about.

It also helps to always have your resume updated and ready to send to any potential new job opportunities that you discover. Be aware of your options and be ready to take advantage of new opportunities that could make a big difference in your career and financial situation.

Working Overtime
One of the easiest ways to earn more income is to work overtime or to ask for extra hours at your current job. This works well if you are already on an hourly basis. If you are a salaried employee, you might be able to arrange some overtime pay beyond your base salary.

Part-Time Job
The next possibility is for you to find a side job that you can do

part-time after work or on your days off. Just an additional day or two, part-time, could really help to reduce your debt or to boost your savings.

Find a Side Hustle
If getting a new job, with a higher salary or an extra part-time job, seems out of the question right now, there's still a lot you can do to boost your income. You just need to find your "side hustle." A "side hustle" is anything you do on the side, even from home, to earn some extra money. Think about the things you know how to do or make that someone else would be willing to pay you to do for them. It is even more fun and enjoyable if your side hustle is also your hobby or passion.

The latest trend in following your passion is to find ways to build a business or earn extra money doing what you like to do or have a special skill to do. Sometimes, what you do on the side, can build into a lucrative enough income flow to replace your main job. Some super successful "side hustles" have even developed into venture capital backed startups. Of course, your "side hustle" doesn't need to be a bigtime startup company to make a big difference to your finances.

There are several simple ways you can boost your income. You can start by doing something that only takes a few hours a week and adds some extra income to your bank account. If you use that extra income wisely to either reduce your debt or build your savings, you will quickly see how a side hustle can fix your finances. There are numerous potential opportunities for you to add some extra income to your bank account.

This is where the possibilities are endless. There are hundreds of things that you could do to earn some extra money to improve your finances. There are numerous gig-websites that help to connect freelancers and side-hustlers with clients looking to hire someone for a specific task. There could easily be something that you do or a skill that you have that someone would be willing to pay you to do for them.

Some of the skills that you can get paid for include:

- Writing (such as blog posts and articles for an agency or a small business that needs some marketing help)

- Editing or proofreading (you can easily get gigs with digital marketing agencies and through online freelance sites like fiverr.com and upwork.com)

- Sell things to people in person and online in direct sales (such as Avon, chloeandisabel.com, Mary Kay, PawTree, Pampered Chef, Amway, SimplyFun, Pink Zebra, etc.)

- Social Media Account Management (check fiverr.com, upwork.com, and digital agencies)

- Designing (logos, stationery, resumes) (check fiverr.com, upwork.com, and digital agencies)

- Website maintenance and updates (check fiverr.com, upwork.com)

- Coaching or consulting

- Tutoring or lessons (check Wyzant, frogtutoring.com, care.com, tutor.com, VarsityTutor.com, etc.)
- Virtual Assistance or secretarial services (check VirtualAssistUSA.com, FreeUp.com, BelaySolutions.com, etc.)

- Computer tech support and programming (check local employment agencies and online tech support providers)

- Dog walking or pet sitting (dogVacay.com, care.com, or start your own service)

- Child care or senior companion care (check care.com. sittercity.com. urbansitter.com etc.)

- PowerPoint Presentations (check fiverr.com, upwork.com)

- Buy & sell – Find interesting underpriced things at a local Goodwill or garage sale and resell for more on ebay, Craigslist, or Facebook Marketplace.

- Translation services (check fiverr.com, upwork.com)

- Market Research – (check Guidepost, Swagbucks, MySurvey.com, Toluna, CashCrate, etc.)

- Art for hire (you can do design work for advertising and digital agencies, also designs for individual customers on deviantArt, ko-fi.com, patreon.com)

- Do something weird, funny, or interesting (on Fiverr.com, people are paid to sing a song, deliver messages, hold up funny signs, videotape messages, wear funny costumes, etc.)

As you can see from a site like Fiverr.com, the possibilities are endless. Whatever it is that you can do, there is probably someone willing to pay you to do it for them. No matter how unusual that might be. So, find YOUR side hustle and start bringing in some extra money to fix your finances.

Chapter 4
Balancing Your Budget

The best way to get control of your financial health is to create and stick to a budget. Balancing a budget can really help you to minimize unnecessary expenses, reduce your debt, and boost your savings. The problem is that most people hate creating and following a budget. Following a budget can be tedious and make you feel like you are denying yourself of things you want. However, a budget doesn't have to be tedious, frustrating, or restrictive. It is more about knowing the truth and making decisions with a clear view of how your spending decisions affect your financial situation.

So, let's do some simple painless things to help you to balance your budget and get a clear picture of ways to reduce your expenses and save more money.

Fixed Expenses
Fixed expenses are bills that are due every month no matter what. They are expenses that you can't control with your day to day spending. Some examples of fixed expenses include: rent, a mortgage payment, insurance (health, home or renters, auto, and life), utilities (even though they can fluctuate), real estate taxes, car payments, and loan payments.

Variable or Flexible Expenses
Flexible expenses are generally things (goods and services) that you purchase and have control over how much you spend. Some examples include groceries, gas, commuting, entertainment, babysitting, clothing, dining out, etc. These are the areas that present the best opportunities for you to reduce your expenses and save more money.

Income

Your income is everything you earn from your employment, government assistance, child support, and side hustles. Anything that adds money into your bank account is an income source for you.

These three main categories (fixed expenses, flexible expenses, and income are what you need to know to help you create and plan a budget that works for you and helps you to improve your financial situation. By knowing where all of your money comes from (your inflows) and knowing everything you spend it on (your outflows) you get a clear picture of what you can do to fix your finances.

So, instead of making a tedious budget and forcing yourself to cut things and stick to restrictive limits, grab some envelopes instead.

On one envelope write INCOME. If you are a couple you can include all of your joint income and expenses for a family budget.

On one envelope write FIXED EXPENSES.

On 10 envelopes write FLEXIBLE EXPENSE _____.

The blank is for you to write what type of expense you have. Here are a few envelopes you can have ready:

- FLEXIBLE EXPENSE – Groceries
- FLEXIBLE EXPENSE – Dining and Carry out
- FLEXIBLE EXPENSE – Entertainment
- FLEXIBLE EXPENSE – Household goods
- FLEXIBLE EXPENSE – Entertainment
- FLEXIBLE EXPENSE – Child, elder, pet care
- FLEXIBLE EXPENSE – Gas, car maintenance
- FLEXIBLE EXPENSE – Medical copays, prescriptions, over-the-counter medicine

At the beginning of the next month, keep a receipt for everything you spend and put it in the correct envelope. If you spend cash or have no receipt, write the expense on a piece of paper and stick it in the appropriate envelope. EVERYTHING that comes out of your savings, checking, or wallet should be noted and placed in the appropriate envelope. Do this for all of your sources of income as well. No matter how small the item (because those small things add up), be sure to include it in the envelope files.

On the last day of the month, gather up all of your envelopes and bank statements and start to complete the following:

MY INFLOWS (INCOME):

Payroll	$_____
Payroll	$_____
Part-time	$_____
Side hustle	$_____
Child support	$_____
Government check	$_____
Interest on savings	$_____
Investment income	$_____
Other _____	$_____
Other _____	$_____
Other _____	$_____
Total INFLOWS:	$_____

MY OUTFLOWS (Fixed Expenses):

Mortgage $_____
Rent $_____
Car Payment $_____
Insurance life $_____
Insurance health $_____
Insurance house $_____
Insurance car $_____
Other _____ $_____
Other _____ $_____
Other _____ $_____

Total FIXED Expenses: $_____

MY OUTFLOWS (FLEXIBLE Expenses):

Groceries $_____
Dining & Carry out $_____
Entertainment $_____
Gas & Car costs $_____
Household goods $_____
Other _____ $_____
Other _____ $_____
Other _____ $_____
Other _____ $_____
Other _____ $_____
Other _____ $_____

Total FLEXIBLE Expenses: $_____

Write your total INCOME here: $_____

Now write your FIXED EXPENSES: $_____

Now write your FLEXIBLE EXPENSES: $_____

Now subtract your FIXED and FLEXIBLE EXPENSES from your INCOME and write the remaining amount here:

$_____

If you have any money left over, good for you. This is money that can be used to reduce your debt or build your savings. If you spent more money then you brought in from your income sources, then that means that you likely used your credit and increased your debt to make ends meet this past month.

If you are satisfied with what you have left after all of your expenses, then there is nothing to worry about. But if you were overbudget or want to save more money, the place to make changes is in the FLEXIBLE EXPENSES section. These are expenses that you have control over. You can eat out less, use coupons, watch movies at home or on Netflix rather than at the theatre, etc. Look at how you spent your money and make a quick list of 5 areas where you can cut some expenses:

1. _____
2. _____
3. _____
4. _____
5. _____

The key to balancing your budget is to know what you are doing with your money, so you can make changes if you really want to.

Chapter 5
Making Your Financial Plan

Now that you have taken some action to improve your credit, reduce your debt, increase your income, and balance your budget, it's time to think about creating a financial plan for your future. Some people think that financial planning is only necessary if you have a lot of money and investments. However, everyone should do some financial planning to protect themselves, their property, and their loved ones.

Here are some of the most important financial protections to have in place as soon as you are able:

- Create a will and keep it updated. Many people think that unless they have significant savings, investments, and other assets that a will is not necessary. If you own ANYTHING, a will is your way of making sure that YOU decide (not a probate court) who gets your stuff if anything happens to you. If you are a parent, your will is a way to let the courts know who you choose to take care of your children, if you die. Otherwise, someone who doesn't know you or your family dynamics will make decisions that could cause you to "turn in your grave." You can contact your local bar association to get a referral to an attorney or legal-aid service to help you create and file your will.

- Review your retirement savings. If you have access to a 401(k) or another retirement plan through work, do your best to save as much as you can in tax deferred accounts to build your retirement nest-egg. If you do not have a retirement plan at work, then you can set up a retirement account on your own. Check the IRS's website on individual retirement account options:

https://www.irs.gov/retirement-plans/ira-online-resource-guide.

- Make sure you have life insurance. Even if you are single, you may want to make sure that a loved one (such as a child, parent, or sibling) is cared for if anything happens to you. It can also save your family the burden of trying to pay for your funeral. If you do have children and a family that depends on you, life insurance is protection that you should do your best to not be without. Get as much or as little insurance that you can afford. If you are short on excess resources, term insurance is the best way to get the most coverage for every dollar you spend. It isn't permanent, and it doesn't build cash value, it is just pure insurance coverage. It also helps to do your research online and to shop for the best value with an A rated insurance company.

- Create a living will, also known as a health directive. This allows you to choose who can make medical decisions about your care if you are injured and incapacitated. You don't want a court or an estranged family member to decide if they should or shouldn't "pull the plug" if you are in a serious and hopeless condition. Decide now, who you trust to have your wishes and best interests at heart. You can also choose someone to make your financial decisions if you are incapacitated, as well. This is called a financial power of attorney. Most financial institutions and hospitals will have some standard forms available for you to use.

- Update your beneficiaries. Sometimes we forget who we listed as our beneficiary when we opened an account. Check all of your savings and retirement accounts and update your records if necessary.

These are the basic things that will assure that your wishes are honored, your loved ones are cared for, and your future is more secure. Of course, if your assets build so that you are ready to do some serious investing, be sure to consult a licensed or registered investment advisor, a tax advisor, and an attorney to guide you through the best solutions to achieve your expanding financial objectives.

www.ingramcontent.com/pod-product-compliance
Lightning Source LLC
Chambersburg PA
CBHW031507210526
45463CB00003B/1115